Cause & Effect: The French Revolution

Robert Green

San Diego, CA

About the Author

Robert Green writes about the politics of Hong Kong and Taiwan for the Economist Intelligence Unit and for Oxford Analytica and regularly reviews books on East Asian subjects. He holds master's degrees from New York University and Harvard University. He enjoys nothing so much as writing about history.

© 2016 ReferencePoint Press, Inc.
Printed in the United States

For more information, contact:
ReferencePoint Press, Inc.
PO Box 27779
San Diego, CA 92198
www.ReferencePointPress.com

LIBRARY OF CONGRESS CATALOGING-IN-PUBLICATION DATA

Green, Robert, 1969-
 Cause & effect : the French Revolution / By Robert Green.
  pages cm. -- (Cause & effect in history)
 Includes bibliographical references and index.
 Audience: Grade 9 to 12.
 ISBN-13: 978-1-60152-796-7 (hardback)
 ISBN-10: 1-60152-796-9 (hardback)
 1. France--History--Revolution, 1789-1799--Juvenile literature. I. Title. II. Title: French Revolution.
 DC148.G695 2015
 944.04--dc23
                                                                2014047678

"History is a complex study of the many causes that have influenced happenings of the past and the complicated effects of those varied causes."

—William & Mary School of Education,
Center for Gifted Education

Understanding the causes and effects of historical events is rarely simple. The fall of Rome, for instance, had many causes. The onslaught of barbarians from the north, the weakening of Rome's economic and military foundations, and internal disunity are often cited as contributing to Rome's collapse. Yet even when historians generally agree on a primary cause (in this instance, the barbarian invasions) leading to a specific outcome (that is, Rome's fall), they also agree that other conditions at the time influenced the course of those events. Under different conditions, the effect might have been something else altogether.

The value of analyzing cause and effect in history, therefore, is not necessarily to identify a single cause for a singular event. The real value lies in gaining a greater understanding of history as a whole and being able to recognize the many factors that give shape and direction to historic events. As outlined by the National Center for History in the Schools at the University of California–Los Angeles, these factors include "the importance of the individual in history . . . the influence of ideas, human interests, and beliefs; and . . . the role of chance, the accidental and the irrational."

ReferencePoint's Cause & Effect in History series examines major historic events by focusing on specific causes and consequences. For instance, in *Cause & Effect: The French Revolution*, a chapter explores how inequality led to the revolution. And in *Cause & Effect: The American Revolution*, one chapter delves into this question: "How did assistance from France help the American cause?" Every book in the series includes thoughtful discussion of questions like these—supported by facts, examples, and a mix of fully documented primary and secondary source quotes. Each title also includes an overview of the event so that readers have a broad context for understanding the more detailed discussions of specific causes and their effects.

The value of such study is not limited to the classroom; it can also be applied to many areas of contemporary life. The ability to analyze and interpret history's causes and consequences is a form of critical thinking. Critical thinking is crucial in many professions, ranging from law enforcement to science. Critical thinking is also essential for developing an educated citizenry that fully understands the rights and obligations of living in a free society. The ability to sift through and analyze complex processes and events and identify their possible outcomes enables people in that society to make important decisions.

The *Cause & Effect in History* series has two primary goals. One is to help students think more critically about history and develop a true understanding of its complexities. The other is to help build a foundation for those students to become fully participating members of the society in which they live.

IMPORTANT EVENTS OF THE FRENCH REVOLUTION

1774
King Louis XVI inherits the throne of France.

1788
Announcement that a national political conference, called the Estates General, will be held in Versailles.

1787
The Marquis de Lafayette returns to France after fighting in the American Revolution.

1790
Members of the clergy are required to take an oath of allegiance to the revolutionary government.

1775   1780   1785   1790

1776
American colonists declare independence from Great Britain and found the United States.

1789
The Bastille, a symbol of oppression, is overrun amid rioting in Paris.

1791
King Louis XVI and his wife, Marie Antoinette, are captured after trying to escape from France, an incident known as the Flight to Varennes.

1792
France declares war against Austria.

1797
Treaty of Campo Formio restores peace between France and Austria.

1799
Napoleon Bonaparte overthrows the Directory and seizes power.

1796
Napoleon Bonaparte is appointed head of the French army in Italy.

1798
The French military invades Egypt.

1795   1796   1797   1798

1815
The Battle of Waterloo ends Napoleon Bonaparte's reign as emperor of France.

1795
A new government, known as the Directory, forms.

1794
The Jacobins fall and Robespierre is executed, ending the Reign of Terror.

1793
Louis XVI and Marie Antoinette are executed by guillotine; the Reign of Terror begins.

Revolution's March

Revolutions have a way of not staying put. Thirteen years before the French Revolution began in 1789, Britain's colonies in North America declared independence and established the United States of America—a republic given birth by revolution. France's king Louis XVI supported the American revolutionaries, and so too did many of his subjects. The French people decided soon after, however, that France too would be better off without a king. "For France, without any question," writes historian Simon Schama, "the Revolution began in America."[1]

Revolution had made the leap from America to France, but it was just getting started. No one knew just where the revolutionary sentiment would lead. Gouverneur Morris, US ambassador to France, captured the wild unpredictability of revolutionary France in a 1792 letter to Thomas Jefferson, who was then serving as the US secretary of state. "On the whole, Sir, we stand on a vast Volcano," writes Morris, "we feel it tremble and we hear it roar but how and when and where it will burst and who may be destroy'd by its Eruptions it is beyond the Ken of mortal Foresight to discover."[2]

Tremors Spread

Tremors of revolution in France reached other nations even as the revolution was still in progress. In the French colony of Saint-Domingue, located on the Western portion of the Caribbean island of Hispaniola, the revolution fueled anger against the French colonial system. French plantations used slave labor to produce coffee and sugar for consumption in Europe. The colony's social inequality was even more blatant than the unfairness in France under Louis XVI, where the top of society grew rich by taxing the common people. Encouraged by revolutionary ideas emanating from France, the slaves rebelled in 1791, and their rebellion developed into a full-scale revolution that drove the French entirely from the island. In 1804 the former colony was reborn as the independent nation of Haiti.

In Ireland, meanwhile, the French Revolution served as a living classroom for rebels opposed to British rule. Wolfe Tone, a leader of the anti-British Society of United Irishmen, took a commission in France's revolutionary army and plotted for a joint insurrection against their common English enemy. The Irish followed the revolution with interest and much sympathy. Tone's peppery speeches had already earned him the nickname "Marat," after Jean-Paul Marat, one of the French Revolution's fieriest orators.

In 1798 France's revolutionary government dispatched a fleet to reinforce Tone's uprising. But tempestuous seas turned back the French fleet. The English crushed the Irish insurrection and hanged Tone. Revolutionary sentiment survived, however, and Ireland became an independent republic in 1922.

> "For France, without any question, the Revolution began in America."[1]
>
> —Simon Schama, historian.

Toward the Present

In Haiti, Ireland, and elsewhere, the French Revolution did much to undermine the logic of empire. Colonies operated on an unequal arrangement of power. Europeans controlled the government, and colonial subjects did the work. The central ideals of the French Revolution—liberty, equality, and fraternity—seemed hard to square with the colonial system.

Yet France held on to many of its colonies for generations after the revolution. Blinded by the glories of their own revolutionary success, the French could not always understand why people did not want to be ruled by France. "The people of 1793 wanted to create a society where all citizens would be free and enjoy equal rights," explains a French journalist. "Myths like these came to be seen as truths and for 150 years French people learnt about the civilizing role that France had in the world."[3]

Resentment among colonial subjects, not surprisingly, festered. In the years after World War II, colonial subjects the world over pressed their own claims for political liberty. Revolutions erupted in Asia, Africa, and Latin America. These struggles for independence, especially in French colonies, often drew inspiration from France's own revolution.

In 1945, for example, revolutionary leader Ho Chi Minh declared the founding of the independent nation of Vietnam, which at the time was still part of the French colony of Indochina. "For more than eighty years," he stated, "the French imperialists, abusing the standard of Liberty, Equality, and Fraternity, have violated our Fatherland and oppressed our fellow citizens."[4] It would take war against France and the United States before Ho achieved his dream of a united Vietnam free of Western interference.

In France as well, the French Revolution provided a template for challenging authority. When radical students marched in the streets of Paris in May 1968, they called themselves "*les enragés*" ("the enraged ones"), after Parisian radicals in the French Revolution. They employed the protest techniques of the revolution of 1789 and seized control of the streets. Nearly everything ground to a halt. Factories shut down. Trains and buses stopped running. It was the biggest strike in France's history.

The guillotine is readied for an execution during the French Revolution's Reign of Terror. Historians still debate why the revolution descended from lofty ideals into a period of tyranny and terror.

But unlike the revolutionaries of 1789, the students were not protesting national bankruptcy, and they were certainly not starving. In a France that had grown rich, they took issue with the soullessness of modern life and mocked their conservative, buttoned-down society. They intended to shock and to be heard. "All that is sacred, there is the enemy,"[5] reads one of their slogans.

The Debate Continues

The revolutionary spirit of 1789 has continued its historical march down to the present, influencing revolutionary aspirations generation after generation. But the revolution refuses to stay put in another way, too. Scholars constantly reinterpret and reinvent the meaning of the French Revolution. In each generation those who write about it tell us something about the revolution but also a great deal about themselves. A historian's contemporary environment inescapably colors his or her interpretation of the revolution.

> "All that is sacred, there is the enemy."[5]
>
> —Student protest slogan from May 1968.

The British author Edmund Burke, for example, revealed a distrust of revolutionary change that was typical of the British reaction while the revolution was ongoing. In the twentieth century, a period of revolution in its own right, the ideas of Karl Marx, communism's chief theorist, influenced academic interpretations of the French Revolution. The French historian George Lefebvre was typical of this trend. In his highly respected work he focused on the role of peasants in French society, abandoning generations of historical emphasis on military and political leaders. His writings influenced a generation of historians.

Today others offer new interpretations, also reflective of prevailing intellectual trends. Each time the French Revolution is reinterpreted, it lives again—and in a different form. "Its influence," writes Lefebvre, "has not yet ceased to play a role in men's lives."[6]

A Brief History of the French Revolution

On May 4, 1789, King Louis XVI, the hereditary ruler of France, presided over a procession of his subjects at his royal residence in Versailles. The occasion was the opening of the Estates General, a national convention that would question the nature of French society and challenge even the king's right to rule the people of France. The three sections of French society, known as the three estates, paraded by the king in order of importance. In the lead was the clergy, the first estate, dressed in their fine robes. Next was the nobility, the second estate, who wore richly colored garments and exercised their hereditary right to carry a sword. Representatives of the common people, the third estate, came last, donning somber black to show their humble station as the least powerful of the three estates.

Gouverneur Morris, an American who would soon serve as ambassador to France, witnessed the ceremony. "The procession is very magnificent, thro a double Row of Tapestry,"[7] he wrote in his diary. Morris was a keen observer of political developments. On that day he noted the coldness of the crowds toward the opulent French queen Marie Antoinette and the gloomy mood of the royal couple. "Neither the King nor Queen appear too well pleased,"[8] Morris wrote.

The king and the queen sat at the top of this hereditary social structure, which determined ranking solely by the chance of birth. The king was a member of the House of Bourbon, one of Europe's great royal families. Like other European monarchs Louis XVI claimed to rule by divine right, meaning that his power flowed from God alone and could not be challenged by his subjects.

In reality, the king's subjects were both unhappy and increasingly willing to challenge his authority. The king was aware of this because he had asked each of the three estates to submit a list of grievances, called *cahiers*, before the Estates General. The grievances revealed a host of competing demands from the three estates. The church, for example, hoped to protect Catholicism as the official religion of France and preserve its traditional exemption from taxation. The nobles clamored for more power in the making of France's laws. But it was the third estate, the common people, who were most dissatisfied with their place at the bottom of French society. They demanded, above all, to be treated equally.

Louis XVI, king of France, claimed he ruled by divine right. He believed that God had granted him the throne and therefore no one could challenge his right to rule.

Meeting of the Estates General

The king called the Estates General in May 1789 in order to air these grievances and to see if the three estates could agree on a program of reforms. It was during the opening procession of this national convention that Morris witnessed the spectacle of the king's unhappiness.

A meeting of the Estates General had not been called in 175 years. Generally, it met only in times of national emergency, and in 1789 Louis XVI called the meeting only because he could think of no better way to address the growing unhappiness of his subjects. He hoped, however, that the convention would be painless, productive, and short. "The King hopes thus to achieve for the nation the most correct and suitable meeting of the Estates," reads a royal statement, "to prevent disputes which might needlessly prolong the duration thereof, to establish essential proportion and harmony in the composition of the three orders."[9]

Despite this conciliatory language, the first day of the Estates General was anything but auspicious. The king met with the representatives of the clergy and the nobility separately from the representatives of the third estate. The third estate was offended, and when the king did meet with them, he received them with silence and required them to file past him in deference. "The King, standing between his two brothers," writes historian Christopher Hibbert, "could not bring himself to address a single word to any of them other than one old man of exceptionally benign appearance to whom he said, 'Good morning, good man.'"[10] In part this was simply the king's manner. He was brusque by habit, but it was a bad beginning nonetheless. The representatives of the third estate were already doubtful of the willingness of the king, the clergy, and the nobility to make concessions that would improve the lives of the common people.

On June 20, 1789, when the representatives of the third estate returned to their usual hall in Versailles where they debated reform, they found it locked and guarded by soldiers. The room was simply being prepared for further negotiations, but the delegates assumed that the king had decided to drive them away empty-handed. Rumors had already been circulating that the king had summoned the army to squash the growing calls for political reform both in Versailles and in the streets of Paris, where people closely followed the events of the Estates General with growing expectations for real change.

The Revolutionary Calendar

After curbing religious influence on political life, French revolutionaries decided to abandon the Gregorian calendar, also known as the Christian calendar. The new revolutionary calendar celebrated the founding of the first French Republic on September 22, 1792, which became day one of Year I.

The new calendar was influenced by the revolutionary craze for decimalization—the practice of using units of ten for currencies, weights, and measures. Ten also became the basis for the new calendar, which divided each month into three ten-day weeks and each day into ten decimal-hour increments, subdivided into one hundred decimal minutes.

Although the number of months remained the same, their names changed. The new names reflected characteristics of either the weather or agricultural events relevant to a particular season. Thus, winter consisted of the three months *Nivôse* (snow), *Pluviôse* (rain), and *Ventôse* (wind). The revolutionaries also discarded the traditional calendar of saints, which identified each day of the year with an important religious figure. The revolutionaries created a new agricultural calendar that celebrated crops and farming implements instead of saints. October 22, 1792, for example, was the *primidi* of Brumaire (the first day of the month of fog) in Year 1 of the Republic of France, and it celebrated the pear.

The ten-day week immediately drew public criticism, both because it lengthened the work week and because the day of rest (formerly Sunday) arrived only three times a month. The calendar was used for twelve years before it was abolished by Napoleon after he became emperor of France.

Uncertain of the meaning of the locked door, the delegates of the third estate sought out a nearby tennis court. There they agreed that no members of the delegation would leave Versailles until the king accepted a new constitution—one that would curb the powers of the king and the privileged classes. This oath, afterward known as the "Tennis Court Oath," proved to be a major turning point in the early days of the French Revolution, for it marked a shift in power away from the hereditary rulers of the country toward the common people of France.

The Bastille Falls

When he discovered that his authority was being openly challenged by the representatives of the third estate, the king was livid. He planned to declare illegal the third estate's decision. Legal or not, the "Tennis Court Oath" was indeed revolutionary. By misunderstanding the significance of a door barred to their delegation, the third estate challenged the established order of power and privilege in France. The demands of the third estate may or may not have survived a direct challenge from the king, but events outside of Versailles were about to drive the revolution at a quickened pace.

Impatient with the results of the Estates General, thousands of commoners in Paris marched into the streets. They attacked nobles, looted the houses of the rich, and demanded arms from the military. The mob ransacked any establishment where they could find swords or rifles. The army was hesitant to confront these citizen soldiers for fear of making the situation worse, but restraint did little to stop them. On the morning of July 14, 1789, a mob gathered beneath the 80-foot (24 m) walls of a much-hated prison called the Bastille. The massive building loomed over its surroundings and over the imaginations of the residents of Paris. Once a fortress, the Bastille had earned its reputation as a prison for political opponents of the king.

It was, in fact, scheduled to be torn down and held only seven prisoners, two of whom were insane and one who was an aristocrat imprisoned by his family to keep him out of trouble. Nonetheless, the mob demanded its surrender, desiring both the weapons and gunpowder inside and a symbolic victory over the government. But the mob was no match for the Bastille's defenses. Eight watchtowers and high walls gave the cannons and sharpshooters a commanding position over the crowd below. Even if the outer wall was breached, intruders would still have to breach the inner wall while exposed to the fire of defenders.

In the end, however, the defenders' resolution was no match for the determination of the mob. Commanded by the indecisive Marquis de Launay, the garrison was hesitant to fire on the mob for fear of further enraging the residents of Paris. Minor battles erupted, and men were shot on both sides, but the Bastille's garrison had no desire to keep up the killing of civilians. In fact, many common soldiers sympathized

Revolutionary France

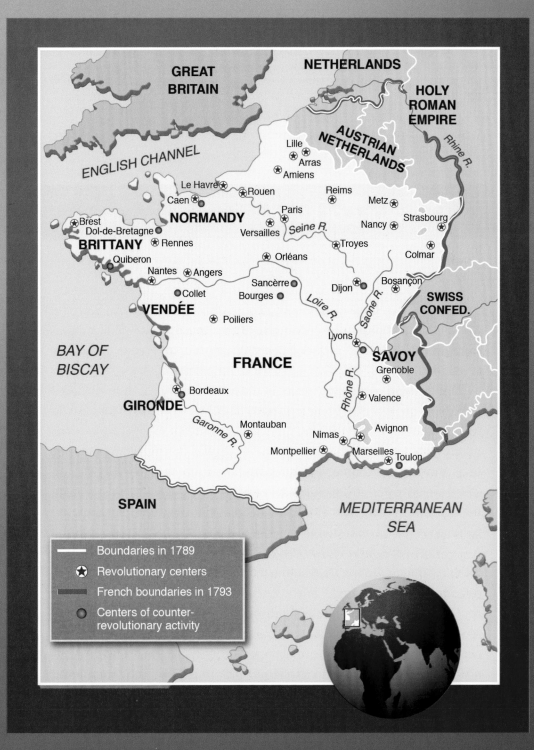

Map legend:

- Boundaries in 1789
- ⊛ Revolutionary centers
- French boundaries in 1793
- ● Centers of counter-revolutionary activity

Map labels:

GREAT BRITAIN

NETHERLANDS

HOLY ROMAN EMPIRE

AUSTRIAN NETHERLANDS

ENGLISH CHANNEL

Rhine R.

Lille
Arras
Amiens
Le Havre
Rouen
Caen
Reims
Metz
NORMANDY
Paris
Nancy
Strasbourg
Brest
Versailles
Seine R.
Dol-de-Bretagne
BRITTANY
Rennes
Troyes
Colmar
Quiberon
Orléans
Nantes
Angers
Sancèrre
Dijon
Bosançon
Collet
Bourges
SWISS CONFED.
VENDÉE
Loire R.
Saone R.
Poiliers
Lyons
BAY OF BISCAY
FRANCE
SAVOY
Grenoble
Bordeaux
Valence
GIRONDE
Garonne R.
Montauban
Avignon
Nimas
Rhône R.
SPAIN
Montpellier
Marseilles
Toulon
MEDITERRANEAN SEA

with the aims of the revolutionaries. "The defection of the army is not one of the causes of the Revolution," writes one observer of events in 1789, "it is the Revolution itself."[11]

De Launay surrendered the fort to the Parisian rabble. He was then paraded through the streets where he was murdered, and his head became a prize of the conquerors of the Bastille. In the following days the building was dismantled stone by stone. July 14 became the defining date of the revolution, and it is still celebrated today as a national holiday in France, known as Bastille Day.

The Tricolor Cockade

The French displayed their sympathy with the revolutionary cause by donning a cockade, a circular badge woven from ribbons. The revolutionary cockade combined the traditional colors of Paris—red and blue—with the white that symbolized the monarchs of the House of Bourbon, a royal family whose members included Louis XVI, the king of France during the revolution.

The inclusion of the king's color in the revolutionary cockade indicated the limited goals of the revolution's early days. The storming of the Bastille represented the end of the king's absolute power, but many were content to retain the king as a figurehead once power was transferred to a revolutionary government. Only three days after the storming of the Bastille, the king traveled to Paris from his residence at Versailles, which sits just outside the city. It was a risky journey into the heart of the revolution, and Louis XVI wrote his last will and testament before setting out.

In Paris, however, order had been somewhat restored by the newly formed National Guard. Its leader was the Marquis de Lafayette, a hero of both the American and French revolutions. As the emblem for his newly organized troops, Lafayette chose the tricolor cockade. When the king reviewed Lafayette's revolutionary troops he agreed to wear the tricolor cockade to show his acceptance of the new political reality. The revolutionary colors are still used in the modern French flag, which is often referred to as the tricolor.

Writing a Constitution

The storming of the Bastille introduced a dynamic that would be repeated throughout the decade of revolution. As politicians attempted to establish a stable revolutionary government, mobs pressed for revolutionary goals through violence in the streets. In the early days these two groups fed off of each other's radical sentiment and kept the revolution moving faster than anyone intended.

Parisian artisans and urban laborers formed the backbone of the mobs. They came to be known as *sans culottes*—those without the fancy short breeches of the aristocracy. Their populist violence soon spread to peasants in the countryside. All over the country, angry commoners looted the homes of aristocrats and smashed symbols of the old order. While this "great fear," as it was described at the time, settled over France, the third estate managed to secure support for a National Assembly that would create the legal framework for a new nation. This new government then set about engineering a radical departure from the *ancien régime*, or former government.

> "The defection of the army is not one of the causes of the Revolution, it is the Revolution itself."[11]
>
> —An observer of the early days of the French Revolution.

Under the new regime the king would be allowed to keep his throne, but he would be a constitutional monarch only—a figurehead with little real power. After deciding to strip the king of his authority, the National Assembly then outlawed France's ancient feudal system. This system organized the land into fiefs presided over by landlords—both landed nobles and wealthy commoners. While the peasants farmed, the nobles managed estates and engaged in the wars of the nation under the banners of their aristocratic families. The peasants, who farmed the lands, owed certain obligations to the landlords, including the payment of burdensome rents. By outlawing the feudal privileges, the National Assembly abolished this system of hereditary land ownership and feudal obligations in a stroke.

Just what, then, would follow? On August 27, 1789, the members of the National Assembly issued the Declaration of the Rights of Man and Citizen. Modeled on the US Bill of Rights, which enshrines revolutionary principles in US law, the document acted as a preamble to France's revolutionary constitution. Among its seventeen points, it declares that "Men are born and remain free and equal in rights."[12] It goes on to stress that political power could be derived only from the nation (not the king) and that all citizens would be equal before the law. It also guarantees the sanctity of property, although fellow revolutionaries continued to busy themselves with looting the property of the rich.

What to Do with the King

France's first revolutionary constitution, one of many to come, was adopted in 1791. The decision to keep Louis XVI in the new government, even in a limited constitutional role, was controversial. Some revolutionaries called for his death, others thought that he should remain but be watched closely to prevent him from undermining the authority of the Legislative Assembly. Having little choice, the king agreed to the demands of the revolutionaries.

Louis XVI, however, remained a pious Catholic. In the early days of the revolution church lands had been seized to finance the government. Just as the nobles had lost their titles and their privilege, the church too was a major target of the revolutionaries. In 1790 the Legislative Assembly demanded that members of the clergy pledge allegiance to the revolutionary government. Clergymen were distrusted, partly because some continued to support the old system, and partly because, as Catholics, their first allegiance was to the Pope, the leader of the Catholic Church, who resided in Rome. When the Pope subsequently denounced the new French government's demand for an oath of loyalty, Catholic priests were forced to choose between France and Catholicism.

"Men are born and remain free and equal in rights."[12]

—Declaration of the Rights of Man and Citizen.

Louis XVI opposed the law requiring the oath, thereby angering the revolutionaries. Fearing for his life, he decided to leave France. On June 20 Louis XVI and the royal family were spirited away in darkness by a lumbering but opulent horse-drawn carriage that belonged to an aristocratic friend. But they were captured near the small town of Varennes. This incident, known as the "flight to Varennes," ended what little goodwill remained for the royal family in revolutionary France.

Soldiers and civilians line the streets of Paris during the return of the French royal family in 1791. Many turned their backs on the royal carriage, a custom usually reserved for funeral processions.

When the king arrived back in Paris, under guard, he was greeted by soldiers and civilians lining the streets in silence, backs facing him in a mock funeral procession. It was bad enough that he had tried to flee, but the revolutionaries thought he was also plotting with aristocrats and foreign governments to restore the monarchy. Accused of being an enemy of the state, he was tried for treason.

The king's dramatic trial produced soaring speeches, mostly calling for his death. In the end he was convicted. On January 21, 1792, his head was lopped off by an execution device known as the guillotine. Henry Essex Edgeworth, an Irish Catholic priest living in France, witnessed the execution. "A sullen silence reigned at first," he writes. "Soon, however, some cries of 'Long live the Republic,' began to be heard. By degrees voices multiplied, and in less than ten minutes (whether from blind rage or cowardly weakness) this cry repeated a thousand times became the shout of the multitude, and all hats were in the air."[13]

A Great Terror Descends

The beheading of Louis XVI shocked many French citizens and many more Europeans abroad. Most of Europe was still ruled by monarchies, and the revolution in France appeared to be spiraling out of control. But the revolutionaries were clear in their motives. The king's execution was intended to discourage those who hoped to restore the monarchy. Maximilien Robespierre, one of the leading revolutionary politicians of the radical camp, summed it up succinctly when he said: "Louis must die because the nation must live."[14]

"Louis must die because the nation must live."[14]

—Maximilien Robespierre, leading revolutionary politician.

Even before the king's trial and execution, the revolutionaries abolished the monarchy. As a result, the people of France were no longer subjects of a monarch but citizens of the first French republic. Chief among the citizens directing the revolution at this stage was Robespierre. He was associated with a group of radical politicians who met in an old Jacobin (Dominican) convent.

The Jacobins, as their political faction was known, attempted to keep the revolution moving forward no matter what the price. Robespierre, a foppish revolutionary who dressed more like an aristocrat, became suspicious of anyone whose commitment to the revolution did not measure up to his own.

In 1793 the Jacobins created the Committee of Public Safety, which acted as a revolutionary police force and court of law used to hunt down and prosecute enemies of the republic. Enemies included clergy and nobles still loyal to the former regime, revolutionaries deemed insufficiently revolutionary, and anyone who was suspected of opposing the Jacobins. "We must rule by iron those who cannot be ruled by justice," Robespierre wrote. "You must punish not merely traitors but the indifferent as well."[15]

This period became known as the Reign of Terror, and it represented the worst excesses of the French Revolution. Packed prisons bred disease and death, while the guillotine dispatched enemies with cruel efficiency. Nearly seventeen thousand people were beheaded. For the crowds the beheadings were intended as both entertainment and warning. Robespierre and the Committee of Public Safety terrified citizens and politicians alike. The terror lasted until 1794 when Robespierre was arrested and the Jacobin clubs outlawed.

The Rise of Napoleon

Sick of the violence and chaos of the terror, the government after Robespierre adopted more moderate policies. Known as the Directory, this new government marked a drift to the right for the revolutionary government. It placed the army in the hands of wealthier revolutionaries and clamped down on the lawlessness of the *sans culottes* and the rural poor. There was even a resurgence of royalist sentiment, as if the blood and terror of the revolution could be undone by a restoration of the House of Bourbon.

The Directory, however, proved unable to rid the nation of challenges from either Jacobins or royalists. Corruption and incompetence ruined its credibility. While the civilian government was flailing, the armies of Republican France marched from victory to victory under the command of a Corsican general by the name of Napoleon Bonaparte.

On November 10, 1799, Napoleon seized power from the Directory, ensuring that the ideals of the French Revolution would not be squandered to royalists or dissipated through weak leadership. Napoleon would continue to spread revolutionary ideas throughout Europe at the head of the French army and the French state, but the decade of the French Revolution was at an end.

How Did Inequality Lead to Revolution?

Focus Questions

1. Since Louis XVI believed that the tax burden on the poor was unfair, why do you think it was so difficult to adopt a fairer tax system?
2. Resentment over taxation played a central role in both the American and the French Revolutions. Why did resentment over taxes boil over into revolution?
3. Had the government distributed food to hungry Parisians, would street violence have been avoided? Why or why not?

Revolutionary sentiment turned France into a hothouse of opinion and resentment. For those who could read, newspapers and broadsheets whipped up anger against the king, the nobility, and the church. Those who could not read listened to explosive speeches or turned to political drawings, which conveyed much with simple, easily recognizable images. In one such image, an elderly peasant, bald and stooped, props himself up with the help of a farming tool. He represents the third estate—the common people who made up 80 percent of France's population. Seated on his back are two splendidly dressed figures, both with satisfied looks on their faces. The first figure seated on the elderly farmer's back represents the clergy, the first estate and the most privileged group in France. The second figure is a nobleman—representing the second estate—identifiable by his sword and his plumed hat. From the pockets of both figures protrude scraps of paper representing the many taxes that the peasants paid to support the clergy and the nobility.

This single image captures the unequal social structure of French society. The royal family sat exclusively at the top of a society that can be imagined as a pyramid of descending powers and privileges. Below the king sat the clergy, which accounted for perhaps 5 percent of the population and owned 10 percent of the land. Below the clergy came the nobles, and finally the wide base of the pyramid represented the remainder of France's population.

While differing widely in social status and political influence, the three estates did not always correspond with wealth. Nobles fallen on hard times were still members of the nobility since the right came from birth. Similarly, commoners grown wealthy through commerce were still members of the third estate. The estates were in fact legal categories that entitled members to certain privileges or obligations. The privileges fell entirely to the first two estates. Only a noble could hunt pigeons and rabbits, for example, even though the peasants complained that both fed on their crops. The obligations fell chiefly on the third estate. And their most important obligation was the payment of taxes.

Taxes Without End

Like the elderly peasant in the political cartoon depicting the three estates, the bottom of society was being crushed by taxation. Taxes were divided into two basic types—direct taxes and indirect taxes. The most basic of the direct taxes was the *taille*, a tax on land that clearly illustrates the inequality of the tax system. First levied in the Middle Ages, this tax was a substitute for military service. Since the nobles held command in the royal armies, they were exempt from the taxes. The clergy also provided services that exempted them from payment. Priests educated students, conducted the Catholic mass, and guided the spiritual life of the French people. Every five years the clergy would donate a certain amount of money to the government as a sign of appreciation for not being taxed. But these donations were voluntary, since the clergy was not required to pay the same taxes as the common people.

It was on the peasants, busy tilling their fields, that taxes fell most heavily. According to the logic of the system, common people were taxed because they did not provide services to the crown—through either military or religious services to the nation. In effect, the *taille* punished the peasantry for doing nothing more useful than growing crops to feed the people of France.

An elderly peasant stoops under the weight of a member of the clergy and a nobleman. The peasant in this 1789 political cartoon represents the common people, who bore the burden of inequality in French society.

The *taille*, however, proved insufficient for the heavy spending of the government. A second direct tax, known as the *capitation*, required payment by individuals regardless of their land holdings. This would have marked a step toward equal taxation, except that many nobles and clergy members secured exemptions by paying a fee to opt out. Still insufficient for government expenses, another direct tax called the *vingtième* required the payment of 5 percent of a taxpayer's salary and was later increased to 10 percent. "If French government in the eighteenth century was of the people, by the king, for the clergy and nobles," writes historian John Hall Stewart, "finances and taxation . . . were at one with the government."[16]

More Taxes Still

A separate type of tax, known as an indirect tax, added to government revenue. These taxes targeted specific items used in daily life. There was a tax on commodities such as tobacco and wine. Yet, the most infamous of these commodity taxes was the tax on salt, known as the *gabelle*. Before refrigeration, salt was used not just to flavor food but also to preserve it. The salt tax fell unequally on different parts of the country. It had already caused at least one uprising in early French history.

These commodity taxes spurred widespread smuggling and a general feeling of unfairness. Originally, all royal subjects were required to pay the commodity taxes, but exemptions were once again given to the clergy and nobles as favors from the crown. Even if all subjects paid the taxes, their bite would be unevenly felt. The rich could easily afford to pay for their salt, but the tax would consume a greater proportion of a poor family's income.

Aside from commodity taxes, there were other demands made on the poor that amounted to a type of tax. The *corvée*, for example, was probably the most disruptive. Although considered a tax, it was actually a requirement to do public work without payment or the right of refusal. The first and second estates were once again exempted, since they viewed manual labor as undignified and beneath their positions in society.

Corvée labor formed the backbone of public works projects, such as the building of roads and bridges. Even the king recognized the inequality of this system, since the poor sacrificed their time and landowners saw a rise in property values from the public works projects. "By forcing the poor man to maintain [the roads] and to give his time and effort without payment of a wage," wrote the king, "we are depriving him of the only resource he has against suffering and hunger in order to be made to work for the profit of the wealthy."[17]

Had Louis XVI been more concerned with the unfairness within France and less concerned with foreign policy, the revolution might never have happened. Instead, new taxes were being considered just before the revolution broke out to make up for the government's mismanagement of public finances.

Empty Coffers

While peasants struggled to meet tax obligations, Louis XVI and his government ministers focused their attention on the international position of France. Rivalries among the monarchies of Europe spurred competition for prestige and overseas empires. Those rivalries often resulted in war. Foremost among the enemies of the French were the British. Of the two, France was both richer and more populous, but the powerful British Navy had spread British influence far and wide.

Britain's American colonies, for example, provided Britain with raw materials, such as timber, fur, and agricultural products. The colonies also provided a market for finished goods manufactured in Great Britain and a source of revenue through taxation. When the American colonists revolted against this system, France seized the opportunity to back the Americans in their struggle against the British.

France's support for the American revolutionaries makes little sense beyond the rivalry between France and Great Britain. The French no more believed in the revolutionary political ideas of the Americans than the British did. Fair taxation, self-government, democracy, and the rejection of the monarchy were, quite certainly, of little interest to the government of Louis XVI. But all of this could be overlooked in order to give the hated British a black eye, so deep was the animosity between the two nations. "It seems to me impossible to be French without wishing ill to England,"[18] remarked France's ambassador to Britain in 1769.

> "It seems to me impossible to be French without wishing ill to England."[18]
>
> —France's ambassador in London.

The American Declaration of Independence in 1776 and the subsequent victory of the Continental Army over British forces was cause for celebration in France. Aiding the colonial struggle, however, had cost France dearly from a purely financial standpoint. Despite the many taxes levied on the third estate, the French government still did not have enough money to support its adventures overseas. It financed support for the American Revolution by taking out loans, often from

An eighteenth-century French bureaucrat collects taxes on salt. People of wealth and status did not have to pay the tax, which angered the citizenry.

international creditors. In fact, France borrowed 90 percent of the money it used for its campaign to deprive England of its American colonies.

The financial condition resulting from the mismanagement of public finances did much to spread the belief that the government could no longer be trusted. "The end of the old regime was the necessary condition of the beginning of a new," writes Simon Schama, "and that was brought about, in the first instance, by a cash-flow crisis."[19]

The king's finance minister, Jacques Necker, was largely responsible for the borrowing, and he argued that France had few other options. Without the loans, taxes would have to be raised once again, and once again they would fall most heavily on the poor. Because of his refusal to raise taxes, Necker became the most popular government minister in the country. For his ruinous borrowing, Necker earned a reputation as a defender of the poor. Louis XVI fired him on July 11, 1789. News of his dismissal enraged mobs in Paris. Three days later these mobs stormed the Bastille, showing the king just what they thought of his government.

Salvaging Privileges

Charles-Alexandre de Calonne, who replaced Necker as finance minister, was supposed to be more sympathetic to the royal court than the populist Necker. After assessing the situation, however, he delivered to the king an unvarnished appraisal of the French economy. "It is impossible to increase taxes, disastrous to keep on borrowing, and inadequate merely to cut expenses," he writes. "The only way to bring real order into the finances is to revitalize the entire state by reforming all that is defective in its constitution."[20]

> "The end of the old regime was the necessary condition of the beginning of a new."[19]
>
> —Simon Schama, historian.

Calonne's reference to "constitution" in this case did not refer to a written legal document but to the nature of the system of government. Louis XVI and his ministers were, however, short of ideas on just how to reform the government to get public finances onto a more sustainable course. The severity of the situation forced the king to agree to some extraordinary steps. He first opened a period of public criticism which allowed the three estates to submit written suggestions for national recovery. These documents, known as *cahiers*, reflected the deep divisions between the third estate and the clergy and nobles.

The clergy sought to protect their historical privileges. The nobles sought to diminish the king's power to expand their own. But the *cahiers* of the third estate provided a window into the simmering resentment in France over the tax system and a social system that allowed the poor to be exploited by the rich. "That such tax be borne equally," records one *cahier*, "without distinction, by all classes of citizens and by all kinds of property."[21]

Although expressed with deference to the king, the demands of the third estate were revolutionary in thought even if not in language. They demanded neither an end to the monarchy nor a political reor-

The Currency of Revolution

To pay the debts run up by the former government, the French revolutionaries turned to a creative finance mechanism known as the *assignat*. This was a bond issued against the value of land seized by the revolutionary government from the church. Fortunately for the revolutionaries, France's creditors accepted this new form of payment. The *assignats* became so common in fact that they began to function as a form of paper currency.

Two factors, however, undermined the stability of the *assignat*. The uncertainty of revolution made land less valuable and consequently lowered the value of the *assignat*. And as values fell, the government printed more *assignats*. The result was a further decline in the value of the *assignat* and a general rise in the prices of goods and, perhaps more important, food. Printing more *assignats* therefore became self-defeating, leading only to inflation and hunger. The government responded with price controls to dampen inflation, but the *assignat* eventually became worthless.

Edmund Burke, a British statesman and political theorist, was highly skeptical that France could sustain its national finances by trading on the value of confiscated land. "Who but the most desperate adventurers in philosophy and finance could at all have thought of destroying the settled revenue of the state," asks Burke, "in the hope of rebuilding it with the materials of confiscated property?"

Edmund Burke, *Reflections on the Revolution in France*, ed. L.G. Mitchell. New York: Oxford University Press, 1993, p. 236.

ganization of the country. But demanding equality under the tax code would logically entail radical political changes.

At the Estates General, the national conference on reform, the third estate forced the issue by demanding the formation of a National Assembly, which they soon dominated. The clergy and nobles scrambled to salvage their place at the top of society by agreeing to more and more reform measures. In other words, the first two estates agreed to give up many of their ancient privileges in order to retain some amount of power in French society. "Their efforts to do so," writes one historian, "developed into a somewhat hysterical renunciation of pre-rogatives, the net result of which was incorporated, during the ensuing week, into legislation. This legislation may be said to have terminated the manorial [feudal] regime of France."[22]

By wresting control of the Estates General and forming a law-making National Assembly, the third estate had turned a debate over public finances into a political reform process that radically altered the nature of French society. By agreeing to some of the demands of the third estate, the clergy and the nobles retained some powers and the king kept his throne. But it was only a temporary victory for the old regime. Questions of economic unfairness were at the same time playing out in the streets of Paris in a much more violent way.

Women and Bread

Inequality in revolutionary France was perhaps most apparent during times of hunger. When food prices rose, the rich simply paid more to keep their bellies full, but the poor often starved. Bread was the staple of the French diet, and the average worker spent as much as half of

An angry group of women, bearing arms, marches to the Palace of Versailles in 1789 to demand bread for the masses. Price increases resulting from a grain shortage had put bread, a staple of the French diet, out of reach for average people.

his income on it. Unlike the rich, most poor people had no extra food stores to tide them over until prices dropped.

In October 1789, while the National Assembly legislated away the ancient privileges of France's aristocrats, a grain shortage in Paris resulted in hunger and growing unrest. This time the bread shortage was not the result of a bad harvest, which was also a common problem. Instead, the bread shortage resulted from a shortage of water, which was necessary for the milling of bread.

> "Sire, we want bread."[24]
>
> —Parisian flower girl to King Louis XVI.

Since women were chiefly responsible for keeping the family fed, they marched into the streets in search of bread. On October 5, 1789, they looted some bakeries and wrecked others that had raised prices to profit from the bread shortage. "In squalid garret, on Monday morning Maternity awakes, to hear children weeping for bread," writes Thomas Carlyle, a British historian. "O we unhappy women! But, instead of Bakers' queues, why not to Aristocrats' palaces, the root of the matter?"[23]

And indeed they did just that. They turned their anger away from the bakeries and toward those responsible for the miserable state of France's economy—the government itself. The women, who had armed themselves with pikes, swords, and other weapons, first marched on Paris's city hall, the Hôtel de Ville, collecting supporters along the way. They then set off for the Palace of Versailles just outside of Paris to put their demand for bread directly to the National Assembly and to the king himself.

After a six-hour march, about six thousand women descended on Versailles carrying their weapons and dragging at least one cannon. In Versailles the king agreed to meet with a single representative of the female uprising. They chose a pleasant-looking, well-mannered girl from a Parisian flower market. "Sire," she said, "we want bread."[24] And then she promptly fainted.

The king immediately ordered food brought to the protesters, but the mood turned ugly. Disbelieving his good will, some of the marchers stormed the palace. As they rampaged through its splendid halls they set upon anyone who tried to stop them. At least two of the palace guards were killed when they tried to interfere, and their heads,

Marie Antoinette

Royal opulence and excess in prerevolutionary France was embodied in a single woman—Marie Antoinette, the French queen. The king was not entirely suited to the role. He was stooped, short-sighted, and not a fashionable dresser. One member of his court said that his manner of walking made him look like a peasant tilling the fields. Besides, he was generally kindhearted and generous.

But his wife was willful, extravagant, and highly opinionated. Worst of all she was foreign. She was the daughter of Emperor Francis I and Empress Maria Theresa of Austria. She became a hated symbol of the inequality of prerevolutionary France. From popular culture sprang a myth that she mocked the starving peasants by saying, "Let them eat cake!" But there is no historical evidence for this. When starving women marched on Versailles in 1789, they attempted to hunt her down and cut her to pieces with their makeshift weapons, but to no avail. The queen had been warned that a mob was on its way and she fled before they arrived.

Revolutionaries later believed that she was plotting with foreign powers to restore the hereditary powers of the French monarchy. She was tried by a revolutionary court and accused of shipping state funds to Austria and all manner of other crimes. She followed her executed husband to the guillotine on October 16, 1793, in the Place de La Revolution, a public square where revolutionaries had torn down a statute of Louis XV and erected the feared guillotine.

fixed at the end of pikes, were soon entertaining crowds outside as they bobbed up and down in celebration.

Marie Antoinette, the queen, who had become a symbol of high living, fled her bed chamber just before the mob broke in. They had missed the queen, but they took out their fury on her room, tearing at the bed with swords and smashing furniture. The hunger march had become an insurrection that threatened the lives of the royal family.

Ultimately, the king and queen presented themselves on a balcony to try to calm the crowds. The royal couple were then forced to march to Paris, where the revolutionaries could keep an eye on them. The entire government, in fact, decamped to the capital. Versailles, a regal symbol of wealth and power, was abandoned by its residents. "Massive iron locks were placed on its gates to discourage looters, and a few guards stood sentry over silent courtyards," writes Schama. "Versailles had already become a museum."[25]

While unfair taxation helped spark the revolution, hunger fueled the desperation of the poor and led them to confront the privileged classes of French society. Indeed, the inequality resulting from the social structure of France and the financial burden placed on the poor became chief drivers of the French Revolution.

How Did the Enlightenment Contribute to the Revolution?

Focus Questions

1. Do you think that Enlightenment ideas would have taken hold in France even without the French Revolution? Why or why not?
2. In your opinion, is there something fundamentally irreconcilable between science and religion? If so, how so? If not, why not?
3. How do human rights exist if they are not protected by the government? Can rights be universal if they are not enjoyed by all?

While a cash-flow problem, as Simon Schama puts it, acted as a trigger, the French Revolution was not driven by economics alone. Demands for bread by the masses and for a fairer tax system by representatives of the third estate marked a revolt against the very ideas that propped up the French monarchy and gave hereditary privileges to the clergy and the nobility. Thought was an essential precursor to action. "Before it was made into law," writes one French revolutionary, "Revolution was made in men's minds and habits."[26]

This reexamination of French society stemmed from an international intellectual movement known as the Enlightenment. The Enlightenment began as a scientific movement in the seventeenth century. Scientists associated with the Enlightenment attempted to explain natural phenomenon—such as Isaac Newton's explanation for the workings of gravity—by observation and the systematic questioning of the nature of things. These scientific principles were then applied to society, which led to new doubts about religion and the traditional social institutions of Europe.

Above all, the enlightenment philosophers believed that the world could be explained through reason. Also known as the Age of Reason, the Enlightenment became a major movement in the history of Western philosophy. "Enlightenment philosophers find that the existing social and political orders do not withstand critical scrutiny," writes one scholar, "they find that existing political and social authority is shrouded in religious myth and mystery and founded on obscure traditions."[27]

Enlightenment thinkers such as Isaac Newton (pictured) inspired a reexamination of French society. The systematic questioning of the nature of things in science led to similar questions about religion and traditional social institutions.

Enlightenment thinkers conducted their debate unrestricted by national boundaries. Scottish and English philosophers influenced French thinkers who in turn helped shape the thinking of Americans in revolt against the British colonial government. The international character of the movement led to a clever description of this forum for ideas as a "republic of letters." Members of this republic of letters questioned the assumption that monarchs had a legitimate right to rule their subjects. While some continued to believe in God, they rejected the idea of the divine right of kings. God in their view did not give authority in this manner—choosing one hereditary monarchy to rule over its subjects with little regard for their wishes.

> "Before it was made into law, Revolution was made in men's minds and habits."[26]
>
> —Unknown French revolutionary.

The Estates General and the Social Contract

The enlightenment swept aside this ancient assumption and replaced it with the belief that a government has the right to rule only if the people give their consent. This idea became known as the social contract. According to Jean-Jacques Rousseau, an Enlightenment hero of the French Revolution, this contract is exercised through a convention of citizens who gather to collectively decide the course of government. Sovereignty—the right to rule—would be legitimate only if it is defined by equals in such a convention. In Rousseau's own words, citizens should "obey no one, but only their own will."[28]

The theory that legitimate government requires the consent of the people heavily influenced the thinking of the representatives of the third estate at the Estates General in 1789. This national convention was called to air grievances in order to avoid a breakdown of society resulting from the failed financial policies of the king and his ministers. As debate proceeded, however, it became clear that the king, the clergy, and the nobles did not intend to abandon their privileges. The third estate responded by putting into action the Enlightenment theories of legitimate authority. As the largest group, they demanded to take control of the reform process by creating a National Assembly, in which their voices would be heard.

They invited the clergy and the nobles to join them in the assembly. The nobles were reluctant, but the clergy was torn between the nobles and the commoners. Bishops and other high church officials tended to side with the aristocracy and defend hereditary privileges. But common priests tended to side with the common people and supported their demand for a National Assembly.

The third estate, in fact, found one of its greatest champions among the clergy. Emmanuel Joseph Sieyès, commonly known as Abbé Sieyès, argued for expanding the political power of the third estate. In a pamphlet called *What Is the Third Estate?*, published during the Estates General, he argues that a legitimate government could be formed only

The *Philosophes* and their Encyclopedia

France's Enlightenment thinkers, known as the *philosophes*, found a literary home in the *Encyclopaedia, or Classified Dictionary of Sciences, Arts, and Trades*. Edited by Denis Diderot and Jean le Rond d'Alembert, the *Encyclopaedia* mirrors the range of interests of Enlightenment thinkers—from science to literature to political theory.

The politically minded *philosophes*, including Montesquieu, Rousseau, and Voltaire, launched attacks against both the monarchy and the church in the pages of the *Encyclopaedia*. The Enlightenment's emphasis on questioning old assumptions through the application of reason brought the publication into conflict with French authorities. Its license to publish, in fact, was revoked in 1759, but it continued to circulate anyhow.

The *Encyclopaedia* provided a movable forum for French intellectual thought and influenced political attitudes in revolutionary France. Its influence reached further still. The French language was widely spoken in eighteenth-century Europe, and the essays of the *Encyclopaedia*, which was issued in installments, circulated widely throughout the continent and beyond. The *Encyclopaedia*, for example, was among the French-language works in Thomas Jefferson's extensive library, which was purchased in its entirety by the US Library of Congress in 1815.

by the common people. "The Third Estate thus contains everything proper to the nation," he writes, "and those who do not belong to the Third Estate cannot be seen as part of the nation. What is the Third Estate? Everything."[29]

His arguments electrified the representatives of the third estate. At the National Assembly the representatives then enshrined in law the Enlightenment principles laid out by Rousseau and Sieyès. On October 1, 1789, for example, the National Assembly issued the *Decree on the Fundamental Principles of Government*, which states that "All powers emanate essentially from the nation [meaning the people] and may emanate only therefrom."[30]

The Enlightenment ideas springing from the republic of letters thus succeeded in overthrowing the ancient idea of monarchy in France and transferred the right to make laws to the common people. Rousseau's theory that "Legislative power belongs to the people"[31] thereby gained the force of law in revolutionary France.

Separating Church from State

The willingness of Enlightenment philosophers to attack the idea of absolute monarchy was matched by their willingness to attack the authority of the Catholic Church. As the first estate, the Catholic clergy was the most privileged section of French society before the revolution. The church had accumulated tremendous wealth from its land holdings, granted by the royal family, and through taxes levied on the common people.

> "What is the Third Estate? Everything."[29]
>
> —Abbé Sieyès, member of the National Assembly.

Abbé Sieyès, born a commoner, used the church like so many other commoners as a vehicle for social mobility. But commoners were not allowed to rise to the top of the church hierarchy. The king selected the church leaders from among the nobility. The discriminatory practices angered commoners, and so too did the church's influence over the government.

There was no separation between the church and the state before the French Revolution, and the church, in fact, functioned as one of the primary influences on government policy, such as the levying of taxes. It used this power to protect its privileged place in society and to

Members of the Estates General air their grievances in 1789. It was hoped that this process would avoid a breakdown of society resulting from the failed policies of the king and his ministers.

exclude other religions. Since 1685 the church exercised a monopoly on religion in France. Only Catholicism was legal.

One of the church's fiercest critics was François-Marie Arouet, better known by his pen name, Voltaire. In spirited prose he attacked both the church's role as a political force and its rejection of religious tolerance. "Of all religions, the Christian is without doubt the one which should inspire tolerance most," he writes, "although up to now the Christians have been the most intolerant of all men."[32]

In a *cahier* representative of the position of the Catholic Church sent to the king before the Estates General, the clergy requested that it should remain unchallenged as the privileged religion in France. The French revolutionaries addressed this question head on in 1789 when the new government issued the "Grant of Religious Liberty to Protestants." This decree allowed for Protestants, the largest religious group

For France's revolutionary government, symbols of the monarchy presented a problem. Statues and paintings of the royal family served as reminders of the power and wealth of the *ancien régime*—the prerevolutionary government under the French monarchy. But the Enlightenment's enthusiasm for cataloguing and classifying presented a promising approach to consigning symbols of monarchy to history.

In 1791 the revolutionary government converted a former royal palace into a public museum known as the Louvre. It opened its doors on August 10, 1793, a year after the establishment of the French republic and the abandonment of the monarchy. In the Louvre the art collection that once belonged to the royal family was pored over by interested commoners and fussed over by curators. Once an artistic celebration of monarchy, the art collection came to symbolize the triumph of reason and celebrated the spirit of human inquiry. The museum's atmosphere of scientific detachment, a hallmark of the Enlightenment, was augmented by the introduction of artwork from abroad, including works captured by France's revolutionary armies campaigning in Europe and in Egypt.

in France after the Catholics, to hold public office and to share in the other rights afforded by the revolutionary government.

Enlightenment thinking, while not always hostile to religion, sought to place man at the center of a rational society. As the French Revolution proceeded, the new government grew increasingly concerned that the church presented a threat to the revolution. They worried that Catholic citizens of France might be more loyal to the pope, the traditional head of the Catholic Church, than to the French government. Rousseau criticized Roman Catholicism for creating this division between loyalty to the state and loyalty to the government, which "subjects [Catholics] to contradictory duties and prevents them from being able to be at one time devout and Citizens."[33]

To prevent a religious challenge to the revolution, the revolutionary government in 1790 reorganized the Catholic Church under a "civil constitution." This made the church reliant on the state both for permission to function and for finances. No longer would the church be allowed to raise taxes directly from the people. When the pope condemned this policy, the revolutionaries demanded that all priests take an oath of allegiance to the state within a week's time or lose their right to hold mass. This "clerical oath," as it is known, resulted in the end of the church's political influence in revolutionary France.

The Idea of Liberty

When French revolutionaries created legal restrictions on the power of the church and the nobility, they were guided by an abstract idea springing from Enlightenment philosophy. This was the idea of liberty, and in the language of the Enlightenment, it generally meant freedom from tyranny. For the French revolutionaries this meant freedom from the arbitrary exercise of power by the king, the church, and the nobles.

The concept of liberty placed the individual at the heart of the state. In revolutionary France the nation was strong if individuals were protected from abuses of power. Liberty from ancient abuses, such as unfair taxation, was the gauge of success.

> "Legislative power belongs to the people."[31]
>
> —Jean-Jacques Rousseau, politically minded Enlightenment thinker.

The French keenly observed the idea of liberty put into political action during the American Revolution. Intellectually, the American and French revolutions sprang from the same philosophical beliefs. One French philosopher, in particular, held enormous sway over the thinking of the revolutionaries in the American colonies. This was Charles-Louis de Secondat, Baron de Montesquieu, known simply as Montesquieu. He explained his ideas on liberty and government in his most influential publication, *The Spirit of the Laws* (1748). The book was much celebrated in both the American colonies and Great Britain, but it was banned in France, where it was seen as an attack on the privileges of the monarchy and the clergy. For Montesquieu, the liberty of a people could be guaranteed only by checks on the powers of government. "The political liberty of the subject is a tranquility of mind arising from the opinion that each person has of his safety,"[34] he writes in *The Spirit of the Laws*.

Ideas in Action

Montesquieu's ideas found expression in the US Constitution, the central legal document of the American republic. The authors of the Constitution, much influenced by the French philosopher, hoped that liberty could be preserved by preventing any single branch of government—executive (president), judicial (courts), or legislative (Congress)—from accumulating too much power.

The success of the American Revolution had a direct effect on the course of revolution in France. America became the laboratory for political experimentation and captured the excitement of advocates for social change in France. Americans, for their part, watched the French Revolution unfold with considerable sympathy. "I say that we have an Interest in the Liberty of France," writes Gouverneur Morris. "The Leaders here are our Friends. Many of them have imbibed their Principles in America and all have been fired by our Example."[35]

That kinship between revolutionaries in France and in America arose from the excitement of putting Enlightenment ideas into action. French volunteers arrived in America with high ideals and a willingness to take part in the battles against the British. Because warfare was the profession of the aristocracy in France, many of these volunteers came from the second estate. They had been exposed to Enlightenment thinking at home, and their time in America made them increasingly revolutionary in their ideas about society.

The Marquis de Lafayette, for example, arrived in America in 1777 at the age of nineteen and was made a major general by the American Continental Army. George Washington, the future American president, treated him like a son, and Lafayette absorbed the idealism of the American colonists. After witnessing the American Revolution's triumph over superior British military forces, Lafayette became convinced that revolution could also succeed in France.

Applying the Lessons

When Lafayette returned to France, he applied the lessons he had learned in America to the political situation in France. After being elected to the Estates General, he sided with the third estate when they demanded the formation of the National Assembly. True to the principles of the Enlightenment, he opposed the hereditary privileges of his own class and believed the king should have only a symbolic role in France's political life. Lafayette in this regard was typical of the moderate revolutionaries who held sway at the outset of the revolution. He favored a constitutional monarchy and the

The Marquis de Lafayette inspects his command of Light Infantry in 1782. While serving with the US Continental Army and witnessing its triumph in the American Revolution, Lafayette became convinced that revolution could also succeed in France.

creation of a legal system that would protect all members of society equally.

Influenced and perhaps aided by Thomas Jefferson, the principal author of the US Declaration of Independence, Lafayette helped author the Declaration of the Rights of Man and Citizen and introduce it to the National Assembly in 1789. This document represents the height of the Enlightenment's influence on the French Revolution. Like the US Constitution, it argues that people's rights in a society come not from government; instead, rights are inalienable from the individual. They exist naturally—and are also called "natural rights"— among all people living under any form of government. The government's job is simply to protect those rights. "The aim of every political association is the preservation of the natural and inalienable rights of man," reads the third of the seventeen points of the declaration. "These rights are liberty, property, security, and resistance to oppression."[36]

This was a revolutionary idea indeed, one common to both the American and French Revolutions and drawn directly from the philosophy of the Enlightenment. Thomas Paine, an Enlightenment thinker whose writings helped stir revolution in America, believed that the American and French Revolutions would spread these ideas all over the globe. In the *Rights of Man*, a book he dedicated to Lafayette, he captures the excitement generated by these revolutionary ideas. "It interests not particular individuals," he writes, "but nations in its progress, and promises a new era to the human race."[37]

The Limits of Enlightenment

Paine's optimism, however, proved to be premature. Enlightenment ideas such as the division of church and state, the jettisoning of hereditary privileges, and equality under the law became lasting parts of both American and French society. But the situations in America and France differed in some fundamental ways. In America, for example, local colonial governments already functioned as legislative bodies, and they were accustomed to hashing out fair solutions through compromise. The American colonists did not seek to overturn their local social order. They had already created a new society in America. Through revolution, the American colonists gained exclusive control over the society that they had already constructed.

Nor did the Americans have to wrestle with the role of the church in the same manner as the French. Religious toleration existed before the revolution simply because of the nature of immigration to North America. A diversity of religious opinion arrived in the colonies because the colonists themselves hailed from different religious traditions in their countries of origin.

In France, the revolution required the complete uprooting of the social structure. The French Revolution outlawed feudalism, toppled the monarchy, and clashed with the Catholic Church, which was a deeply important institution for many French people. The revolution caused violent shocks to French society, and as a result it lacked the moderation of the American Revolution. "A nation so poorly prepared to act independently could not attempt total reform without total destruction,"[38] writes Alexis de Tocqueville, a French aristocrat who much admired the moderation of the American Revolution.

The distinction between the two revolutions perhaps boils down to Montesquieu, who managed to convince Americans to divide power between three branches of government but failed to convince his own countrymen. As a result, reason and fairness, trumpeted by the Enlightenment philosophers, was slowly abandoned as the French revolutionary government grew greedy for power. By 1792 Lafayette, described as the "hero of two worlds" for his role in the revolutions in America and France, was fleeing France on horseback. His arrest had been ordered by increasingly radical revolutionaries, and France was descending into a period of revolutionary terror.

How Did the Revolution Result in a Reign of Terror?

Focus Questions

1. Do you think that capital punishment is ever acceptable? Why or why not?
2. Why do you think the French Revolution was so much bloodier than the American Revolution?
3. Is violence ever justified as a means to gain political rights? If so, under what conditions? If not, why not?

From the fall of the Bastille in 1789 to the end of the revolution in 1799, violence marched hand in hand with revolution. Political persecution, rebellion, and war with France's European enemies led to a state of unrelenting conflict. "From the first year it was apparent that violence was not just an unfortunate side effect from which enlightened Patriots could selectively avert their eyes," writes one historian, "it was the Revolution's source of collective energy. It was what made the Revolution revolutionary."[39]

But historians still debate why the French Revolution descended from lofty Enlightenment ideals into a period of tyranny and terror. Three factors in particular appear to have guided the revolution toward a bloody phase known as the Reign of Terror. First was a general rise in fear—the fear of enemies abroad and of wavering revolutionary loyalty among French citizens. The second was the struggle among the revolution's leaders for control of the government. The third was the lack of checks on the power of the revolutionary government. Without anyone to stop the paranoia of France's revolutionary leaders, the nation spiraled into self-destructive violence.

Waves of Fear

War acted as an engine for the revolution from its very beginning. The debts incurred by Louis XVI's support for the American Revolution helped ruin France's finances and spark revolution. But war nearer home threatened France in a more direct way. Monarchs still held sway over the rest of the continent, and the overthrow of the French monarchy was by nature threatening to the other European monarchs. In April 1792 France declared war against the Austrian Empire and sent armies marching into the Austrian Netherlands (present-day Belgium and Luxembourg).

French aristocrats and other supporters of the king who had fled France during the revolution added to the danger for the revolutionary government. Known as *émigrés*, these royalist exiles (among them the king's brother) plotted to restore Louis XVI to his full powers and undo the revolution. They held war councils outside France's borders, generally in Germany and England. The revolutionary government had already demanded their return by January 1792, but few found that an attractive prospect. The French government therefore seized their lands and declared them enemies of the state, an offense punishable by death.

The outbreak of war with Austria exacerbated fears that the exiles would march on France side by side with the foreign troops. The nervous government called up troops to fight its European enemies. Just three months after declaring war, news reached Paris that the commander of the Austrian forces, the Duke of Brunswick, had drafted an incendiary declaration with the help of an exiled French aristocrat, the Marquis de Limon. The declaration, known as the Brunswick Manifesto, promised that Paris would be burned to the ground if the French royal family was not protected by the revolutionary government. It provided a spark in the explosive atmosphere and proved suspicions of conspiracy between foreign powers and French opponents of the revolution. "Two great movements," writes British historian Thomas Carlyle, "agitate this distracted National mind: a rushing against domestic Traitors, a rushing against foreign Despots. Mad movements both, restrainable by no known rule."[40]

To Arms!

The Brunswick Manifesto triggered an immediate reaction in Paris. Mobs stormed Paris's city hall and created a radical city government known as the Commune. These *sans culottes* then marched on the Tuileries, a royal palace that was serving as the seat of the revolutionary government and the Parisian home of the king. When the mob reached the palace, the king's contingent of Swiss guards opened fire. The marchers returned volley for volley, killing over five hundred of the Swiss guards.

The king took refuge with the National Assembly, but it was of no use. He was now a prisoner, and his fate would be decided by a national convention tasked with salvaging the revolution amid the quickly spreading chaos and fear. "The atmosphere in Paris was now suddenly transformed," writes Christopher Hibbert, "as ambassadors were withdrawn by their governments, the salons closed their doors, and aristocrats, who, though stripped of their titles, had previously been left in peace provided they were not suspected of being counter-revolutionaries, thought it as well to leave their houses and go into hiding."[41]

> "There are some Seven Prisons in Paris, full of Aristocrats with conspiracies."[42]
>
> —Thomas Carlyle, Victorian historian.

Some of the aristocrats who did not go into hiding fell victim to mob violence. The *sans culottes* then raided the prisons of Paris looking for enemies of the revolution who had been locked up by the revolutionaries. "There are some Seven Prisons in Paris," writes Carlyle, "full of Aristocrats with conspiracies."[42] The mob murdered about half of the prison population. Their victims included political prisoners, clergymen, aristocrats, and common criminals.

"A Terrible Beauty Is Born"

This phase of violence against the old order also resulted in the arrest of the king and the queen. They were stripped of their titles and given the surname Capet, a name taken from French kings of old. They became the most famous of France's prisoners and awaited trial as Mr. and Mrs. Capet, enemies of the state.

In the meantime, a national convention was called to set up a new French government that, for the first time, included no monarch. On September 22, 1792, the convention proclaimed Year 1 of the Republic of France, known to history as the First French Republic, since

The severed head of King Louis XVI of France is held aloft for all to see after his execution by guillotine in 1793. Though the monarchy had fallen, a period of tyranny and terror was about to begin in France.

subsequent republican governments have risen and fallen since the days of the French Revolution.

In what would become a template for justice under the revolutionary government, the king was tried by a court of revolutionary politicians. Members of the government did not defer to judges and courts but took it upon themselves to determine the guilt of their political enemies. If there was any single mechanism of government that could be held responsible for the terror that descended on France, it was the system of political trials. Guilt and innocence were not determined by evidence but solely by the political views of the accused. Among the accusations against Louis XVI was one that stated he had "caused the blood of Frenchmen to spill."[43] The court sentenced him to die by guillotine. Upon his death the government proclaimed, "[Citizens,] the tyrant is no more."[44]

The overthrow of the king and the founding of the First French Republic are sometimes described as the second French Revolution. The founding of the republic represented the height of antimon-

In the days after the fall of the Bastille, a French revolutionary named Jean-Paul Marat stirred public passions through his newspaper *The Friend of the People.* His fiery writings became more violent and more radical as the revolution progressed. He excited public sentiment by calling for the heads of aristocrats, priests, and counterrevolutionaries.

As if this enemies list was not long enough, Marat also turned on fellow revolutionaries. He was especially distrustful of the Girondist faction, with whom his own faction, the Jacobins, initially had much in common. But despite being fellow revolutionaries the Girondists opposed Marat's bloodthirsty calls for political violence. They were particularly alarmed by a massacre of political prisoners in Paris and other parts of France in September 1792. It was a massacre that Marat had urged on in the pages of his newspaper.

A Girondist supporter named Charlotte Corday held Marat responsible for the persecution of the Girondist faction. On July 13, 1793, she arrived at Marat's house in Paris with a knife concealed within her clothes. Corday stabbed Marat to death while he soaked in a medicinal oatmeal bath used to treat a skin condition. The brutish-looking Marat was transformed by the painter Jacques-Louis David into a romanticized martyr in his painting *The Death of Marat.* Corday had no regrets. "I killed one man to save a hundred thousand; a villain to save innocents," she said before the blade of the guillotine silenced her.

Quoted in Thomas Carlyle, *The French Revolution: A History.* New York: Modern Library, 2002, pp. 648–49.

archist achievement. The revolution had rid France of the political influence of Catholics, and now it buried the monarchy in an act of violent retribution. The poet W.B. Yeats describes the violent rise of Irish nationalism with the words, "A terrible beauty is born."[45] The French now had their own terrible beauty—a republic of equal citizens born from blood and violence. And it was about to become more terrible still.

The Committee of Public Safety

The execution of the king earned for France the enmity of the other monarchs of Europe. But the revolutionary government met foreign criticism with defiance. "The kings in alliance try to intimidate us," said Georges-Jacques Danton, an increasingly powerful member of the government. "We hurl at their feet, as a gage of battle," Danton said, "the French king's head."[46]

The rise and fall of Danton, one of the most famous of all the revolutionaries, is illustrative of the course of the Reign of Terror, a phase of the revolution that unfolded in the years 1794 and 1795. Danton became a leading member of the Jacobins, the most radical of all factions in the government. At the National Convention this faction seated itself on elevated benches far from the center of the proceedings. As a result, they earned the nickname "the Mountain."

The Jacobins soon seized control of the revolutionary government, and Danton became their most effective speaker. It was noted by those who heard Danton that his manner of speaking was the only thing more ferocious than the scowl on his intense heavyset face. His calls for war with the monarchs of Europe were answered by the National Convention in 1793, when France declared war on England and Spain. War, however, threw the government into a desperate position. It needed to call up troops, wage war abroad, and keep an eye on enemies of the revolution at home.

To handle these urgent needs, the National Convention voted to create the Committee of Public Safety—an executive body of nine members. The committee effectively became the government of France during the Reign of Terror. Danton took the helm and set out to restore order in France by using increasingly harsh measures. The government had already authorized execution for those who hoarded food or sought to profit from food sales. Danton now advocated for expanded punishments for enemies of the revolution as well. He championed the Revolutionary Tribunal, which was used to prosecute political opponents and reign in mob violence. Danton reasoned that if the state prosecuted opponents of the revolution, the violence in the streets would stop. "Let us be terrible," he said, "so that we can prevent the people from being terrible."[47]

In the Shadow of the Mountain

In the beginning, however, the Committee of Public Safety under Danton combined harsh laws with sincere attempts to make peace with revolutionary factions that opposed the Jacobins. In particular, he tried to resolve a split with the Girondists. Hailing from the southern department (administrative region) of Gironde, these Jacobin revolutionaries disagreed with the Jacobins over the fate of the king in revolutionary France. Many Girondists were constitutional monarchists, and others simply felt that executing the king damaged France's reputation.

> "Let us be terrible, so that we can prevent the people from being terrible."[47]
>
> —Georges-Jacques Danton, revolutionary leader.

The Girondists were also shocked by street violence, promoted by radical Jacobins in the government and in the press. They believed that the use of violence as a political weapon would undermine the credibility of the revolutionary government. Danton approached the Girondists in 1793 to try to smooth over differences between the two factions. He was rebuffed, however, and a vicious struggle erupted between the two camps. "Gironde and Mountain are now in full quarrel," wrote Carlyle. "All these men have the word Republic on their lips; in the heart of every one of them is a passionate wish for something which he calls Republic, yet see their death-quarrel!"[48]

The Mountain proved the stronger of the two factions, and the Committee of Public Safety unleashed its vengeance on the Girondists, hunting them down and prosecuting them for the crime of disagreeing with the Jacobin point of view. Paris became a fearful place as agents of the government scoured the city for Girondists. Even Thomas Paine, an American revolutionary who had been made a French citizen and supported the Girondin faction, was temporarily imprisoned. The Girondist leader, Jacques Pierre Brissot, and other prominent leaders died at the Place de la Revolution, the Parisian square used for public executions.

The elimination of the Girondist faction increased the powers of the Jacobins. This power increasingly was exercised through the Committee of Public Safety. Danton's influence, however, was waning. He spent much of his time negotiating with France's European enemies to

Imprisoned Girondists debate their own future and the future of France. Members of this group split with other revolutionaries. They criticized the use of violence as a political weapon and favored a limited but continuing role for the king.

put an end to the costly military campaigns. During his absence from Paris the revolution found a new champion—Maximilien Robespierre.

Champion of Terror

Robespierre, finicky and foppish, was a lawyer by trade. While the masses had adopted trousers and workmen's clothes as an outward display of revolutionary virtue, Robespierre continued to powder his hair and dress in the knee breeches favored by genteel society before the revolution. Despite his aristocratic air, he rose to prominence solely through merit, marshalling logical arguments in legal cases with great success.

Contemporaries described the peculiar greenish hue of his skin, which affected even the whites of his eyes. As if embracing this otherworldly air, he preferred green for the color of his clothes. Humorlessly, he plotted his way to power with a cool and calculating intellect. "He had virtues and vices as neatly catalogued as a confessor's manual," writes one biographer. "He saw all life like a chess board, in black and white squares, and no neutral colors."[49]

While Danton doubted the wisdom of persecuting political enemies, Robespierre had no such scruples. He became the standard of revolutionary virtue, embodied in a single man. Those who were accused of being enemies of the state were measured against the ruthless dedication of Robespierre himself. Robespierre, in particular, turned on his rival for leadership in the committee. In March 1794 Danton was arrested and accused of pilfering money intended for France's European diplomatic initiatives. His closest political allies were also arrested, lending an air of persecution to the affair. At his trial no evidence was produced nor a single witness called. Allowed to speak on his own behalf, Danton displayed his famed ability to win the sympathy of the audience.

Annoyed by the spectacle, Robespierre had the trial cut short, and Danton was condemned to die. On the day of execution Danton first witnessed the beheading of his friends and political allies. He was then marched to the blood-stained platform where the guillotine awaited. Crowds gathered to see the end of the famous revolutionary. Executioners had developed a grim custom of raising aloft the heads of famous people to make the crowds cheer. "Make sure you show them my head," Danton said, defiant to the last. "It will be worth it."[50]

> "Anybody who expressed dissenting opinions was assumed to be an enemy of the people—thus the horrifying logic of the Terror."[51]
>
> —Sylvia Neely, historian.

Enough Is Enough

In the months after the execution Robespierre concentrated more and more power into the hands of the Committee of Public Safety, in part by expanding the government's power to prosecute enemies. In 1794 a new law set up revolutionary tribunals that would be used by Robespierre in his witch hunts. Lawyers would no longer be given to de-

56

Revolutionary leader Maximilien Robespierre is arrested shortly before his execution, in July 1794. At the height of his power, all citizens were viewed as potential enemies of the state. In Paris alone, beheadings reached an average of thirty a day.

fendants, and witnesses would no longer be called during trials. People lived or died on their ability to prove their loyalty to the revolutionary government.

For the guilty the only sentence allowed was death. Trials became daily revolutionary theater under Robespierre. Beheadings sped up to an average of thirty a day in Paris alone. All citizens were potential suspects. "Anybody who expressed dissenting opinions was assumed to be an enemy of the people—thus the horrifying logic of the Terror," writes historian Sylvia Neely. "It could not be stopped because if you showed doubts about it, those doubts were proof that you were a traitor or in the pay of the enemy."[51]

Danton's execution, however, proved to be the first step in the undoing of Robespierre. If a hero of the people and a towering figure of the revolution could be deemed an enemy, how could anyone be safe?

Guillotine

The excessive cruelty of the French Revolution is perhaps best represented by a single device—the guillotine. Condemned prisoners were placed horizontally on a wooden plank with their necks beneath a heavy, angled blade suspended in the air. On the executioner's command the blade dropped, and off came the head.

This might seem like a gruesome idea today, but at the time it was considered an advancement in the treatment of prisoners condemned to death. Previously, prisoners were lashed to wagon wheels and beaten, inflicting first pain and then death. The guillotine was intended to deliver only death, swiftly and painlessly. It was designed, in fact, by a doctor named Antoine Louis and was known for a time as a *louisette*.

The more common name is derived from a fair-minded reformer named Joseph-Ignace Guillotin, who argued that all persons condemned to death should face the same treatment. Priests, nobles, and commoners all met their end by the thousands during the revolution. The guillotine also took the heads of King Louis XVI and his wife, Marie Antoinette. It was used most enthusiastically during the Reign of Terror, during which Robespierre condemned both supporters of the former regime and fellow revolutionaries before he was himself executed by guillotine in 1794. The use of the guillotine outlived the revolution. It was used for the last time in 1977, and the death penalty in France was abolished four years later.

Other members of the government grew worried that Robespierre and the Committee of Public Safety would turn on them next. The public mood turned against Robespierre as well, and shouts of "tyrant" could be heard when he walked in the streets.

In July fellow Jacobins struck. Robespierre was declared an outlaw, and his arrest was ordered. He attempted to escape capture by jumping from a window but succeeded only in breaking both his legs. He later tried to avoid the guillotine by shooting himself, but he earned himself only a painful wound in his jaw.

Robespierre still had many followers among the people of Paris, however, and he hoped that they would march on the government once again to save him. "The only salvation for the Robespierrists lay in armed insurrection of the Parisian populace—a step that hitherto had never failed," writes one historian. "This time it failed, and the Revolution had run its course."[52] In late July 1794 Robespierre met the same punishment that he had dealt out to so many others. He was guillotined in the Place de la Revolution. It turned out not to be the end of the revolution, but it spelled the end of the revolution's bloodiest chapter. It was the end of the Reign of Terror.

How Did the French Revolution Lead to the Rise of Napoleon?

Focus Questions

1. Do you think that compulsory military service like the *levée en masse* is justifiable in times of war? Why or why not?
2. Since the Directory was unpopular and undemocratic, was it justifiable for Napoleon to seize power? Explain your answer.
3. After proclaiming himself emperor of France, was it possible for Napoleon to continue to spread revolutionary ideas? Explain your answer.

France's military campaigns played a crucial role in the French Revolution from its very beginning. Louis XVI's support for the American Revolution had nearly bankrupted the state. During the ten years of the French Revolution, there was not a single year when French troops were not battling enemies at home or beyond France's borders. "War changed the nature of the revolution," write historians Robert Tombs and Isabelle Tombs, "and the revolution changed the nature of war. France's revolutionary leaders—especially now that they were regicides [king killers]—were literally fighting for their lives: against the foreign invader, against the royalists within, and even against each other, as failure or weakness could mean death."[53]

By 1793 France was at war with European enemies in every direction—with Spain to the south, Austria and the independent German kingdom of Prussia to the east and northeast, and with independent Italian kingdoms to the southeast. The British, meanwhile, threatened the coast of France from both the Atlantic and the Mediterranean with their powerful navy. The revolutionary government was particularly fearful of conspiracies between foreign powers and French royalists, who hoped to restore the French monarchy and put an end to the revolution.

The danger of such cooperation was made clear in July 1793, when royalists seized the coastal city of Toulon. Located on a strip of coast that jutted out into the Mediterranean, Toulon was a vital French port and the site of a major arsenal and considerable timber supplies for building France's navy. When royalists seized the city, about a third of the French Navy lay at anchor in the harbor. To hold the city against a counterattack by revolutionary forces, the royalists appealed to the British and Spanish, who dispatched soldiers packed into warships.

The revolutionary government at once dispatched troops by land to dislodge the joint force of French royalists and foreign soldiers. When the revolutionary forces neared Toulon, they witnessed the king's old flag fluttering above buildings in the city. Even worse, the British had hoisted their own flag above the arsenal. Revolutionary troops surrounded the port, and for four months they chipped away at the defenses.

Artillery proved to be the decisive weapon. And a twenty-four-year-old artillery officer made his name during the battle—training his hilltop guns on the royalists hunkered down in the city below until their defenses finally broke. This was Napoleon Bonaparte, barely 5 feet 6 inches (1.7m) in height but destined to become a towering figure in French history.

> "War changed the nature of the revolution, and the revolution changed the nature of war."[53]
>
> —Robert Tombs and Isabelle Tombs, historians.

Revolt in the Vendée

The French Revolution increasingly came to rely on military men like Napoleon to keep enemies at bay. Even without foreign intervention, French citizens opposed to the dramatic changes brought on by the revolution threatened to topple the revolutionary government. A rebellion that broke out in the same year as the siege of Toulon—in a region known as the Vendée—revealed the depth of support for both the royal family and the church by opponents of the revolution. The area, located in Western France, abuts the Atlantic Ocean and the Loire River valley. Life in the Vendée revolved around agricultural seasons and customs more suited to the feudal past that was abolished at the outset of the revolution.

Napoleon Bonaparte, pictured leading an attack on British forces in 1793, became a towering figure in French history. He first made a name for himself in a battle against French royalists who had seized the coastal city of Toulon.

The immediate cause of the uprising was a law passed in August 1793. The law required that all administrative regions of France, known as departments, raise troops for the nation's wars. Called the *levée en masse* in French, the law amounted to conscription, or the mass mobilization of the population for military service. "The young men shall go to battle," the decree states. "The married men shall forge arms and transport provision; the women shall make tents and clothes, and shall serve in the hospitals."[54] Even children and the elderly were asked to pitch in.

While the world has since seen wars, such as World War II, in which entire populations participated in the war effort, this was unheard of at the time. "It represents the first complete wartime mobilization of a nation in modern history," writes John Hall Stewart, "and reflects the zealous spirit current in France."[55]

That spirit may have been widespread among revolutionaries, but in the Vendée it was not. In fact, the zeal of the revolutionaries to fight foreign enemies was matched by the zeal of the peasants of the Vendée to fight the government. Collecting makeshift weapons, the people organized the Catholic and Royal Army and set out to rid the area of Jacobins and any other revolutionaries they could find. "The announcement of the recruiting levies," writes Simon Schama, "turned all this pent-up anger and resentment into outright revolt."[56]

Revolutionary troops in the area were routed by this zealous army of traditionalists. In response, the government organized a military expedition and set out to crush the rebellion. Both sides killed with abandon, but the rebels were no match for the regular troops of the national army. The Catholic and Royal Army therefore resorted to guerrilla warfare, striking at the enemy and retreating into the countryside that they knew so well. Fighting under their slogan "God and king," the rebellion lasted until the end of the French Revolution in 1799, and flared up even after.

"A Whiff of Grapeshot"

The uprising in the Vendée rekindled fears of cooperation between royalist forces and the armies of France's foreign enemies. The British, in fact, had helped to smuggle in French royalist exiles and supplied royalist rebels with arms and money in the Vendée and elsewhere. The temporary success of the Vendée uprising had also convinced the royalists that they could succeed only if they seized the entire country, otherwise government forces would regroup and stamp out local resistance. "Once they were committed to civil war," explains Schama, "there was no avoiding that much broader strategic goal."[57]

Government policy during the Reign of Terror also proved to be an excellent recruiting tool for the royalist cause. The Jacobins had alienated many French citizens. Both the persecution of political enemies and the revolutionary government's hostility toward the church

In 1798 Napoleon Bonaparte, France's most celebrated general, landed in Egypt after a string of military victories in Europe. He had slipped past a British fleet scouring the Mediterranean looking for French ships to sink. In Egypt he hoped to disrupt British communications with India, the crown jewel of the British Empire. But the real legacy of the expedition would be a momentous advance in scholarship.

Travelling with Napoleon were 150 of France's most distinguished academics and artists. Known as the savants, these men of learning hailed from the French Institute, a center of learning established in Paris by the revolutionary government. In Egypt these savants established an Egyptian Institute and set about discovering the wonders of Egyptian civilization. While studying Egypt's monuments the scholars longed to read the hieroglyphs, the curious pictographic writing of the ancient Egyptians. The meaning of these symbols had been forgotten for centuries, even among the Egyptians.

In 1789 Napoleon's troops stumbled on an invaluable clue. While fortifying defenses near the town of Rosetta, French soldiers unearthed a stone tablet that later came to be known as the Rosetta Stone. It included the same message written in three different scripts—ancient Greek, demotic (a type of Egyptian script), and hieroglyphs. By comparing the different forms of writing, a French scholar named Jean-François Champollion deciphered the meaning of the message and cracked the code to reading hieroglyphs in 1822.

offended segments of the French population. Even former supporters of the revolution wondered if France might be better off without the murderous policies of the Committee of Public Safety. After the government beheaded Robespierre and banned the Jacobins in 1794, royalists decided to strike while the new government was just finding its feet.

On October 5, 1795, as royalist forces neared Paris revolt broke out in neighborhoods where royalist feeling still ran high. In the Tuileries, a former Bourbon palace, the government scrambled to gather enough troops to put down the revolt. The situation was desperate, and some in the government feared a complete collapse of the republic.

Napoleon, the hero of Toulon, had the good fortune of being in Paris at the time. He was given command of troops around the Tuileries, the seat of the government. He turned once again to his artillery, just as he had done in Toulon. Other commanders hesitated to attack Parisian citizens even though they were in revolt, but Napoleon had no such qualms. His cannons ripped through royalists as they marched toward the government. A few hundred people were killed, but Napoleon later claimed that the ferocity of the initial barrages did much to save life, since it broke the rebellion with, in the words of Thomas Carlyle, "a Whiff of Grapeshot."[58]

For crushing the revolt Napoleon was elevated to the rank of general. He became a national hero and the protector of the new revolutionary government formed just three weeks later, known as the Directory.

Napoleon crushed a royalist revolt at the Tuileries Palace in 1795, where three years earlier he had witnessed the storming of the palace by thousands of French citizens (pictured). He became a national hero and, for his efforts, was elevated to the rank of general.

The Directory

Representing the final phase of revolutionary government, the Directory guided the French Revolution through its final five years. It attempted to provide stability after chaotic years of political infighting, beheadings, and civil war. "The Directory attempted to provide a stable and liberal form of government, which would preserve the moderate social gains of the Revolution," writes historian Martyn Lyons, "but would avoid a repetition of the repressive violence and tyrannical dictatorship associated with the Terror."[59]

The Directory replaced the National Convention, which Robespierre and the Jacobins had controlled through committees. The new government was divided into two legislative bodies, the Council of Five Hundred and the Council of Elders. The first body would propose legislation, and the second held only the power of veto. Executive powers were exercised through a body of five directors, who were elected by the Council of Elders. Power was thus divided between the legislative and executive branches of government but concentrated in the five-member Directory.

The new government quickly set out to undo some of the more unpopular laws adopted during the terror. It restored, for example, the rights of a defendant to a professional legal defense. Under the Directory the courts would no longer be used to persecute political enemies. "Since many of them were lawyers," writes Lyons, "the provision of a just legal system and a humane penal code were vital preoccupations."[60]

The aim of the Directory was to calm a nation that had experienced unimagined trauma through civil war and revolutionary terror. The Directory era began with great promise. "People who had resented the burden of being forced to be virtuous and who felt oppressed by life under a regime of fear now experienced an overwhelming sense of relief,"[61] writes Sylvia Neely.

For the first time in the revolution a certain gaiety returned to the streets of Paris. Fancy dress displaced the working-class clothes of the *sans culottes*, formerly favored as the uniform of revolution. A sense of snobbery returned to Paris as well. The young paraded in stylish outfits and frittered away their time gambling and dancing. Foppishly dressed young men even wandered the streets attacking Jacobins and *sans culottes* with heavy walking sticks and smashing statues of revolutionary leaders.

Napoleonic Code

The French Revolution left a permanent mark on the legal system of the modern world. In 1804 Napoleon Bonaparte adopted the *Code civil des Français,* or the French civil law code, more commonly known as the Napoleonic Code. This code sought to preserve, through the legal system, many of the revolution's ideals—most notably the equal treatment of all people before the law.

Among the world's legal systems the civil code has a powerful competitor—formulated by the traditional rival of the French. This is the system of English common law. While the Napoleonic system draws on the example of written law handed down from the Roman Empire, the English common law system is more of a patchwork affair. It draws on local customs and the precedents of earlier cases. The role of judges differs markedly in the two systems. In English common law previous rulings, known as precedents, direct the decisions of a judge. In the Napoleonic system rulings are based on written guidelines, known as civil codes.

English common law took root in countries that had a historic connection to Great Britain, such as Australia, Canada, and India. Similarly, the Napoleonic code spread with French conquest and colonization. In the United States, English common law holds sway, except in one state—Louisiana, named for King Louis XIV of France. Formerly a part of New France, France's North American colonies, Louisiana to this day uses a civil code system based on Napoleon's revolutionary legal reforms.

The Problem with Elections

It quickly became clear that the Directory represented, above all, the interests of the bourgeoisie—well-to-do professionals whose financial interests required stable government. They sympathized with neither the royalists, who used to lord it over them, nor the *sans culottes* whose street violence they feared. As a result of the favoritism they showed to people of their own class, the leaders of the Directory were popular with very few people in France.

Citizens made plain their dislike of the Directory in the 1797 elections for members of the Council of Five Hundred and the Council of Elders. The constitution required elections for a third of the council seats. In the election Royalists trounced supporters of the republic (and the Directory) in overwhelming numbers. Intended to demonstrate legitimacy, the first open elections under the Directory instead revealed a complete lack of confidence in the government.

Fearful of being crushed between royalist support and Jacobin revolutionaries, the Directors turned to the army for help. With the backing of the army, they were emboldened to void the election results on September 4, 1797, in what became known as the coup d'état of Fructidor, after the Revolutionary Calendar. Since they were opposed to guillotining political enemies in the fashion of the Jacobins, the Directory simply exiled them to France's far-flung colonies.

Elections the following year gave the Directory the opportunity to show equal contempt of the opposite end of the political spectrum. With the royalists cowed and exiled, the Jacobins this time emerged victorious while the moderate council candidates supportive of the Directory gained little public support. The Directory responded once again by nullifying the election results and packing the government with its own supporters. Effectively this proved to be a second coup d'état, referred to as the coup of Floréal.

> "People of Italy! The French army comes to break your chains."[63]
>
> —Napoleon Bonaparte.

Spoils of War

The Directory by this point was entirely discredited. It was also broke. Poor harvests, continual war, and empty state coffers resulted in a financial situation as desperate as the one that had brought on the revolution. But the Directory had an ingenious, if highly unscrupulous, solution to this problem. For much of the revolution, war strained state finances. But under the leadership of Napoleon war was turning a profit.

Grateful for Napoleon's clearing the streets of royalists in 1795, the Directory had appointed Napoleon commander of France's Army of

Parisians, dressed in the latest fashions, walk along one of the city's famous boulevards in 1798. Under the new government known as the Directory, gaiety returned to the streets of Paris.

Italy. At the head of this army, Napoleon set off on a highly profitable military campaign. In 1796 he took over an exhausted and underpaid army facing fortified passes through the mountains blocking entry to northern Italy. "Soldiers," he addressed them, "I seek to lead you into the most fertile plains in the world. Rich provinces, great cities will be in your power. There you will find honor, glory, and riches."[62]

Napoleon, an engine of restless energy, first sent out troops as a diversion, then skirted the fortified passes with his main force and rapidly descended onto the plains of Italy. Next, he set about conquering the divided states of Italy and breaking the will of the Austrian forces that were helping to deny conquest to the French. Revolutionary fervor lent his campaign an air of moral authority. "People of Italy!" he pronounced. "The French army comes to break your chains."[63]

In place of principalities and monarchies, he left new republics founded on the principles of the French Revolution. But his interest in conquest had a more practical aspect, too. Whatever peoples he liberated he immediately taxed. He used these funds to pay his troops and diverted the remainder to the Directory. Napoleon's conquests thus became the main source of funds for the cash-strapped government. And the French general, who preached liberty, spent much of his time looting the treasures of Italy. "Since one must take sides, one might as well choose the side that is victorious, the side which devastates, loots, and burns," Napoleon said rather cynically. "Considering the alternative, it is better to eat than to be eaten."[64]

The Month of Fog

After years of conflict at home, Napoleon's victories gave the French something to celebrate. "We have drowned its earlier shame," Napoleon said of the revolution, "in floods of glory."[65] But controlling the source of France's revenues, its army, and the goodwill of the people made of Napoleon a force more powerful than the government itself.

In October 1797 the Austrian monarchy buckled from constant French military pressure. France and Austria signed the Treaty of Camp Formio, which drove Austria from parts of Italy, Belgium, and other European territories. When Napoleon returned to Italy he returned as a conquering hero. In the popular imagination he was the personification of the ideals of the revolution.

The Directory, in the meantime, had descended even further into corruption and repression. Holding the middle ground between royalists and Jacobins required greater repression, harsher laws, and even less popularity for a government that had never known the goodwill of the people it governed. "When this liberty collapsed into anarchy," writes historian Robert Gildea, "the obvious solution was recourse to dictatorship by a general thrown up by the revolutionary armies who were establishing France as a Grande Nation in Belgium and the Netherlands, the Rhineland, Switzerland and Italy."[66]

While the general public heaped praise and adulation on Napoleon, politicians feared him for just this reason. When he returned to France he was met with rumors that he intended to rule as dictator. Hoping to get him out of the country, the Directory encouraged him to lead a French fleet across the English Channel and invade England. "The Channel is a ditch that will be crossed when someone has the boldness to try it,"[67] he said. But instead he sailed for Egypt, where he could threaten British trade routes to India, at the time a prized British colony.

> "When this liberty collapsed into anarchy, the obvious solution was recourse to dictatorship by a general."[66]
>
> —Robert Gildea, historian.

The Directory breathed a sigh of relief. They were no match for Napoleon. But it only delayed the confrontation. He returned in 1799, and in November, the month of fog according to the revolutionary calendar, he seized control of the French government. He appointed himself consul, modeled on the rulers of the ancient Roman Republic, but within a span of five years he had himself crowned emperor of France. His coup against the Directory marked the end of the French Revolution and the rise of the age of Napoleon. He would, in the words of Alexis de Toqueville, "both continue and destroy the Revolution."[68]

Introduction: Revolution's March

1. Simon Schama, *Citizens: A Chronicle of the French Revolution*. New York: Vintage, 1989, p. 24.
2. Gouverneur Morris, *A Diary of the French Revolution*, vol. 2. Boston: Houghton Mifflin, 1939, p. 449.
3. Quoted in Martin Evans, "French Resistance and the Algerian War," *History Today*, vol. 41, no. 7, July 1991. www.historytoday.com.
4. Ho Chi Minh, *Declaration of Independence of the Democratic Republic of Vietnam*, 1945. https://chnm.gmu.edu.
5. Quoted in libcom.org, "Slogans of 68." https://libcom.org.
6. Georges Lefebvre, *The French Revolution: From Its Origins to 1793*. New York: Columbia University Press, 1962, p. xviii.

Chapter One: A Brief History of the French Revolution

7. Morris, *A Diary of the French Revolution*, vol. 1, p. 66.
8. Morris, *A Diary of the French Revolution*, vol. 1, p. 66.
9. Quoted in John Hall Stewart, *A Documentary Survey of the French Revolution*. New York: Macmillan, 1961, p. 27.
10. Christopher Hibbert, *The Days of the French Revolution*. New York: William Morrow, 1980, p. 49.
11. Quoted in Sylvia Neely, *A Concise History of the French Revolution*. New York: Rowman & Littlefield, 2008, p. 76.
12. Quoted in Stewart, *A Documentary Survey of the French Revolution*, p. 114.
13. Henry Essex Edgeworth, *A Narrative of Remarkable Occurrences Connected with the Death of Louis XVI*. Montreal: Nahum Mower, 1812, p. 28. https://archive.org.
14. Quoted in Neely, *A Concise History of the French Revolution*, p. 169.
15. Quoted in Hibbert, *The Days of the French Revolution*, p. 225.

Chapter Two: How Did Inequality Lead to Revolution?

16. Quoted in Stewart, *A Documentary Survey of the French Revolution*, p. 77.
17. Quoted in Alexis de Tocqueville, *The Ancien Régime and the Revolution*, trans. Gerald Bevan. New York: Penguin, 2008, p. 179.
18. Quoted in Robert Tombs and Isabelle Tombs, *That Sweet Enemy: Britain and France, the History of a Love-Hate Relationship*. New York: Vintage, 2006, p. 150.
19. Schama, *Citizens: A Chronicle of the French Revolution*, p. 62.

20. Quoted in Neely, *A Concise History of the French Revolution*, p. 45.
21. Quoted in Stewart, *A Documentary Survey of the French Revolution*, p. 77.
22. Stewart, *A Documentary Survey of the French Revolution*, p. 106.
23. Thomas Carlyle, *The French Revolution: A History*. New York: Modern Library, 2002, p. 211–12.
24. Quoted in Hibbert, *The Days of the French Revolution*, p. 225.
25. Schama, *Citizens: A Chronicle of the French Revolution*, p. 470.

Chapter Three: How Did the Enlightenment Contribute to the Revolution?

26. Jonathan Israel, *Revolutionary Ideas: An Intellectual History of the French Revolution from the Rights of Man to Robespierre*. Princeton, NJ: Princeton University Press, 2014, p. 15.
27. William Bristow, "Enlightenment," *The Stanford Encyclopedia of Philosophy*. plato.stanford.edu.
28. Jean-Jacques Rousseau, *Of the Social Contract or Principles of Political Right & Discourse on Political Economy*, trans. Charles M. Sherover. New York: Harper & Row, 1984, p. 30.
29. Abbé Sieyès, *What Is the Third Estate?* (1789), reproduction, University of Wisconsin, Eau Claire. http://open.uwec.edu.
30. Quoted in Stewart, *A Documentary Survey of the French Revolution*, p. 115.
31. Rousseau, *Of the Social Contract or Principles of Political Right & Discourse on Political Economy*, p. 52.
32. Voltaire, "Tolerance," in *The Philosophical Dictionary*, trans. H.I. Woolf. New York: Knopf, 1924. http://history.hanover.edu.
33. Rousseau, *Of the Social Contract or Principles of Political Right & Discourse on Political Economy*, p. 128.
34. Montesquieu, *The Spirit of the Laws*, University of Virginia Library Digital Curation Services. http://etext.lib.virginia.edu.
35. Morris, *A Diary of the French Revolution*, vol. 1, p. 60.
36. Quoted in Stewart, *A Documentary Survey of the French Revolution*, p. 114.
37. Thomas Paine, *Rights of Man*. Ware, UK: Wordsworth Classics of World Literature, 1996, p. 119.
38. Tocqueville, *The Ancien Régime and the Revolution*, p. 166.

Chapter Four: How Did the Revolution Result in a Reign of Terror?

39. Schama, *Citizens: A Chronicle of the French Revolution*, p. 447.

40. Carlyle, *The French Revolution: A History*, p. 513.

41. Hibbert, *The Days of the French Revolution*, p. 169.

42. Carlyle, *The French Revolution: A History*, p. 529.

43. Quoted in Stewart, *A Documentary Survey of the French Revolution*, p. 391.

44. Quoted in Stewart, *A Documentary Survey of the French Revolution*, p. 392.

45. W.B. Yeats, *The Poems*. New York: Macmillan, 1989, p. 180.

46. Quoted in Hibbert, *The Days of the French Revolution*, p. 193.

47. Quoted in Hibbert, *The Days of the French Revolution*, p. 195.

48. Carlyle, *The French Revolution: A History*, p. 607.

49. J.M. Thompson, *Leaders of the French Revolution*. New York: Harper Colophon, 1929, p. 234.

50. Quoted in Graeme Fife, *The Terror: The Shadow of the Guillotine, France 1792–1794*. New York: St. Martin's, 2006, p. 303.

51. Neely, *A Concise History of the French Revolution*, p. 219.

52. Crane Brinton, *A Decade of Revolution, 1789–1799*. New York: Harper & Row, 1934, p. 193.

Chapter Five: How Did the French Revolution Lead to the Rise of Napoleon?

53. Tombs and Tombs, *That Sweet Enemy*, p. 205.

54. Quoted in Stewart, *A Documentary Survey of the French Revolution*, p. 473.

55. Stewart, *A Documentary Survey of the French Revolution*, p. 472.

56. Schama, *Citizens: A Chronicle of the French Revolution*, p. 700.

57. Schama, *Citizens: A Chronicle of the French Revolution*, p. 704.

58. Carlyle, *The French Revolution: A History*, p. 772.

59. Martyn Lyons, *France Under the Directory*. New York: Cambridge University Press, 1975, p. 3.

60. Lyons, *France Under the Directory*, p. 4.

61. Neely, *A Concise History of the French Revolution*, p. 222.

62. Quoted in Stewart, *A Documentary Survey of the French Revolution*, p. 672.

63. Quoted in J. Christopher Herold, *The Age of Napoleon*. Boston: Houghton Mifflin, 2002, p. 53.

64. Quoted in Herold, *The Age of Napoleon*, pp. 8–9.

65. Quoted in Herold, *The Age of Napoleon*, p. 60.

66. Robert Gildea, *Children of the Revolution: The French, 1799–1914*. Cambridge, MA: Harvard University Press, 2008, p. 5.

67. Quoted in Tombs and Tombs, *That Sweet Enemy*, p. 242.

68. Tocqueville, *The Ancien Régime and the Revolution*, p. 204.

Books

Nonfiction

William Doyle, *The French Revolution: A Very Short History*. New York: Oxford University Press, 2001.

Paul Hanson, *Historical Dictionary of the French Revolution*. New York: Rowman & Littlefield, 2015.

Felix Markham, *Napoleon*. New York: Signet, 2010.

Peter McPhee, ed., *A Companion to the French Revolution*. Hoboken, NJ: Wiley-Blackwell, 2014.

Dorinda Outram, *The Enlightenment*. New York: Cambridge University Press, 2013.

Jeremy D. Popkin, *A Short History of the French Revolution*. Upper Saddle River, NJ: Pearson, 2009.

Timothy Tackett, *When the King Took Flight*. Cambridge, MA: Harvard University Press, 2004.

Fiction

Georg Buchner, *Danton's Death*. London: Bloomsbury Academic, 2011.

Charles Dickens, *A Tale of Two Cities*. New York: Penguin, 2011.

Voltaire, *Candide, or Optimism*, trans. Theo Cuff. New York: Penguin, 2009.

Websites

French Revolution Digital Archives (http://frda.stanford.edu). Primary-source documents and images collected by Stanford University Libraries and the Bibliothèque Nationale de France.

French Revolution: How Did the British React to July 1789? (www .nationalarchives.gov.uk/education/resources/french-revolution).

Excerpts from contemporary newspaper accounts recording British opinions on the French Revolution.

Liberty, Equality, Fraternity: Exploring the French Revolution (http://chnm.gmu.edu/liberty-equality-fraternity-exploring-the -french-revolution). An interactive resource guide created by George Mason University.

Marie Antoinette (www.pbs.org/marieantoinette/index.html). A timeline, photos, and information about Marie Antoinette's role in the French Revolution.

Napoleon (www.pbs.org/empires/napoleon). An interactive guide to the rise and fall of France's most famous general.

78